R~~eflections on the~~
Mysteries of the Rosary

Mark G. Boyer

LITURGICAL PRESS
Collegeville, Minnesota

www.litpress.org

Cover design by Joachim Rhoades, O.S.B. Photo courtesy of Getty Images.

Nihil obstat: Robert C. Harren, *Censor deputatus.*
Imprimatur: ✠ John F. Kinney, Bishop of St. Cloud, May 17, 2005.

ISBN 13: 978-0-8146-3015-0
ISBN 10: 0-8146-3015-4

2	3	4	5	6	7	8

Library of Congress Cataloging-in-Publication Data

Boyer, Mark G.
    Reflections on the mysteries of the Rosary / Mark G. Boyer.
      p. cm.
   ISBN 0-8146-3015-4 (alk. paper)
  1. Mysteries of the Rosary.　　I. Title.

BT303.B69　　2004
242'.74—dc22

2004007632

Dedicated to
Rev. Msgr. Jerome Neufelder,
1929–2002,
priest, spiritual director, friend

Contents

The Glorious Mysteries

Introduction

This little book provides reflections for each of the four Mysteries of the Rosary: Joyful, Light, Sorrowful, and Glorious. It is intended to be used as a set of guided reflections for those who pray the rosary. One can return to its reflections repeatedly in order to gain deeper insight to the mysteries being prayed.

Each two-page reflection provides the title of the mystery, a verse from Scripture, and a reflection that provides background to understanding the biblical text, an application for life in the twenty-first century, and a suggested focus for the reader in making a personal application of the reflection as he or she meditates on and prays the specific decade of the rosary.

"Rosary" comes from a Sanskrit word meaning "garden of flowers" or "necklace of beads." "Bead" comes from an Anglo-Saxon word meaning "prayer." Thus, the rosary is a garden of prayer. Like any garden, to grow hearty and strong, sun, rain, and fertilizer are needed. These reflections serve as the sun-rain-fertilizer-meditation for the garden of prayer, the rosary. Hopefully, the pray-er will return to them again and again to foster the growth of many prayer-flowers in his or her life.

It is easy to pray the rosary. While touching the cross, one makes the sign of the cross and says the Apostles' Creed. Then going to the first large bead, he or she says the Our Father, followed by three Hail Marys, one on each of the three small beads, and a Glory Be. On the next large bead, the first mystery is announced, after which one reads the biblical verse and the reflection from the appropriate section of this book. When finished, one says an Our Father and ten Hail Marys, counting them on the first set of ten small beads, while meditating upon an application of the reflection in this book. One may linger on each Hail Mary as he or she focuses his or her attention on how the mystery being prayed is lived by the pray-er. At the end of the decade the Glory Be is prayed. On the next large bead announce the next mystery and proceed through each successive decade as indicated above. After praying all five mysteries, say the Hail, Holy Queen prayer.

Traditionally, the Joyful Mysteries are prayed on Monday and Saturday; the Mysteries of Light on Thursday; the Sorrowful Mysteries on Tuesday and Friday; and the Glorious Mysteries on Sunday and Wednesday. However, when using these reflections, pray-ers may choose to say only one decade a day from a Mystery and meditate deeply upon its application in his or her life. Or one may choose to space the five decades and their reflections throughout the day, such as early in the morning, mid-morning, noon, mid-afternoon, and evening.

It is the writer's hope that this little book will deepen reflection and meditation of those who use it while praying the mysteries of the rosary.

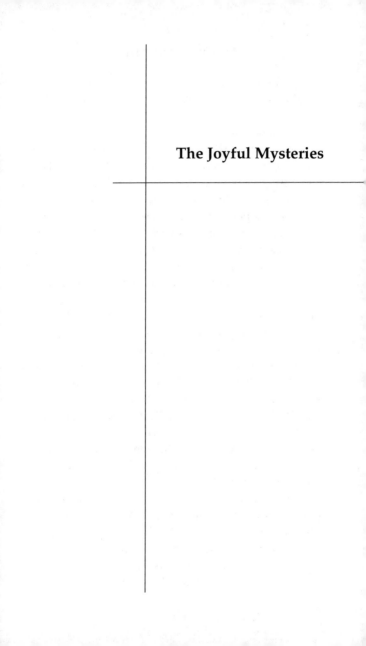

The Joyful Mysteries

The Annunciation

[Gabriel announced to Mary,] "You will conceive in your womb and a bear a son, and you will name him Jesus." (Luke 1:31)

Every major event culminates in an announcement of some kind. Ancient kings of long-forgotten cities recorded the announcement of the defeat of their enemies on clay tablets, papyrus scrolls, and parchment sheets. Sometimes they erected a stele or an arch to serve as a perpetual announcement concerning the event. Egyptian pharaohs kept a scribe at hand at all times, just in case they might make an announcement of desert-shaking proportions.

Both the author of Matthew's Gospel and the author of Luke's Gospel think that the imminent birth of Jesus deserves a similar announcement. So, Matthew's angel of the Lord—an Old Testament code for God—speaks to Joseph in a dream and announces that his fiancée, Mary, has conceived through the Holy Spirit and she will give birth to a child whom Joseph will name Jesus. Luke portrays the announcement more formally. The angel Gabriel—meaning "God's strength"—announces to Mary that the Holy Spirit will come upon her and God's power will overshadow her and she will give birth to a Son of the Most High God, a Spirit-child, who will be named Jesus.

The practice of ancient kings and pharaohs and gospel writers continues today. A graduation from high school or college is usually announced through the mail with an invitation. The imminent union of a man and a woman is announced as an engagement in the Sunday newspaper. It will appear there again as a wedding announcement. Family and friends of the bride and groom will receive wedding announcements. The announcement of a baby shower precedes the annunciation of the birth. And most newspapers contain an obituary section announcing the deaths of members of the community.

Announcements come into our lives from God, too, all the time. While they may not be accompanied by an angel, God announces new ideas to us through our reading. Watch a movie, and God might announce something important to you through one of the characters. Listen intently to a spouse or friend, and you might hear God give you the solution to a problem. When your conscience dictates what you know to be the right thing to do, when you speak the truth, when you accept full responsibility for your actions, be assured that you are hearing announcements from God.

As you pray this mystery, reflect on some of the recent announcements that you have received from God. Be joyful that God continues to announce good news to you.

The Visitation

"Mary set out and went with haste to a Judean town in the hill country, where she entered the house of Zechariah and greeted Elizabeth." (Luke 1:39-40)

If we visit an ill friend in the hospital, we think of ourselves as the visitor. Likewise, if we visit a relative in a nursing home, we consider ourselves to be the visitor. Those involved in hospice care know that they visit and care for those who are near death. Furthermore, when we visit, we may bring a magazine, a plant, or cookies to someone. Certainly, we carry concern and conversation to the person we visit.

In Luke's unique story of Mary visiting Elizabeth, we at first conclude that Mary is the visitor and Elizabeth is the visited, and on the surface level, that is true. Mary has journeyed to Zechariah and Elizabeth's home to see them. But Mary has already been visited by God in the person of Gabriel. So, as she proceeds to visit Elizabeth, she discovers that God has not only already visited Elizabeth, too, but that Elizabeth serves the role of visitor, also. This means that she receives Mary as the mother of the Lord, and she shares the good news that has been entrusted to her, namely, that she has been filled with the Holy Spirit, bears the Lord's forerunner—John the Baptist—in her own womb, and that there are plenty of God's blessings to go around. In other words, the visitor, Mary, becomes the visited, and the visited, Elizabeth, becomes the visitor.

We live in a culture that dictates that we measure our worth by how well we visit others. Mary and Elizabeth lived in a culture that measured hospitality in terms of what was received from others. Instead of approaching a friend in the hospital with the preconceived idea that you are the visitor and he or she is the visited, try making your visit one in which you are open to receive from the ill person. Likewise, when visiting a relative in a nursing home, focus on what you receive from the elderly or handicapped. Even though you may make the trip, those who have suffered, those who have lived, those who have loved have many gifts to offer to their visitors.

For example, by listening to the words of the elderly, you might discover a solution to your problem. By listening to the sick, you might discover the power of suffering. By listening to children, you can understand truths that used to be unintelligible. We never know when our visit to another may turn out to be a visit of the other to us. After all, God is always the first to visit us during prayer when we may actually think we are visiting God. Ask Mary. Ask Elizabeth.

As you pray this mystery, reflect on some of the recent visitations that you have received from others and God when you thought you were doing the visiting. Be joyful that God continues to visit you.

The Nativity

[Joseph] took [Mary] as his wife, but had no marital relations with her until she had borne a son; and he named him Jesus. (Matt 1:24b-25)

There are many points of view from which to describe the affects a birth has on other people. A doctor delivering a child would narrate the story from a birthing procedure point of view and tell how it followed usual medical protocol or taxed the doctor's knowledge of medicine. The father of the child would tell it from the perspective of coaching the mother, his wife, and how much effort he had to put forth to keep her focused on the task at hand. The mother's point of view would probably begin with the end of her nine-month pregnancy and work backward to the time of conception. If the child could talk, he or she would explain what it is like to be evicted from a warm home after only nine months of residency, to be forced through a canal toward bright lights, and to promptly have every orifice suctioned before being washed and wrapped in a blanket.

Matthew and Luke each tell of Jesus' nativity from the point of view of how his birth will affect other people. Matthew is concerned with Jesus' birth from a Gentile perspective, featuring a story about the Magi arriving at Joseph and Mary's house with funerary gifts of gold, frankincense, and myrrh for the child. According to Matthew's Gospel, Jesus came to gather both Jews and Gentiles into God's reign above the heavens before he died. Luke chooses to explain how Jesus' birth will affect the poor, represented by the shepherds, who are the first to come and see the child in a manger. The shepherds serve as a sign of all the outcast and unclean of the first century. According to Luke, Jesus came to call tax collectors, prostitutes, the demon-possessed, and the rest of humankind's social misfits to share God's reign.

Your birth has affected a lot of people. Your parents might tell your nativity story from the point of view of the great changes you made in their lives. Your grandparents would tell the story from the perspective of a new grandchild and all they wanted to do for you. How would your preschool and kindergarten teachers tell the affect you had on their lives? What point of view would your elementary principal choose? How about your high school classmates? What affect have you had on your friends? We often make it through a lifetime and never take time to think about all the people whose lives we have touched and affected.

As you reflect on this joyous mystery of the nativity of Jesus and how his birth affected his world, examine your birth from the point of view of the ways you have affected the people who inhabit your world.

The Presentation

When the time came for [Joseph and Mary's] purification according to the law of Moses, they brought [Jesus] up to Jerusalem to present him to the Lord . . . . (Luke 2:22)

An introduction of one person to another can more accurately be called a presentation. One person says to another, "John, may I present to you Mary." And the other responds, "I am pleased to meet you, Mary." The French usually respond with *"Enchante,"* meaning "I am enchanted or pleased to meet you." During an elegant ball, daughters of prominent citizens are presented to members of a country club. During the halftime of a football or basketball game, the nominees for homecoming queen and their escorts are presented both to former and current students in a high school.

In Luke's unique story, Jesus is presented in the Temple by Joseph and Mary. The Spirit-conceived child in effect is brought to his Father's house where he is presented to God. As Luke narrates the story, two elderly and wise people recognize and explain the meaning of Jesus' presentation. First, Simeon, filled with the Holy Spirit, declares that Jesus will be a light both for Jews and Gentiles. In other words, Jesus is presented to all people. Second, Anna speaks about the redemption of Jerusalem that will be accomplished through Jesus. In other words, all will be saved through Jesus. The legends of Simeon and Anna betray a characteristic of Luke's style throughout his Gospel, namely, the careful balance of a story about a man with one about a woman.

Simeon and Anna represent the wisdom of the older years. There is something about age that knows, that recognizes truth, that can discern the deep-down certitude of things and share it with others. Most of the time we associate wisdom with grandparents, who instruct their grandchildren in truths that parents cannot seem to communicate. In our culture, mentors serve the same purpose; they take young men and women and explore with them the issues that really matter to them: relationships, love, life, spirituality, sex, and death. Teachers are also dispensers of wisdom; there are instructors who give more than course materials. They inspire learning that lasts a lifetime instead of memorizing what is quickly forgotten.

As Simeon and Anna make clear, God presents the Holy One's wisdom through people. God can be recognized in countless presentations if we but open our eyes and hearts, like Simeon and Anna. As you pray this mystery, reflect upon all the truth and joy that has come to you from God through others who have been presented to you.

The Finding in the Temple

After three days [Joseph and Mary] found [Jesus] in the
temple, sitting among the teachers, listening to them and
asking them questions. (Luke 2:46)

The only canonical story of Jesus as a boy is found in
Luke's Gospel. Jesus is twelve years old. He and his
parents have just been to Jerusalem for Passover, the
annual celebration of Jewish liberation from Egyptian
bondage. Mary and Joseph think that their child is
with others on the return trip, but he has stayed in
Jerusalem where, after three days, they find him in the
Temple. Of course, this account of Jesus being found in
the Temple is meant to parallel his presentation in the
Temple. The author has even crafted similar endings
for both stories. As Luke portrays Jesus, the Spirit-
child, being presented to God in the Temple in the pre-
vious story, in this one he portrays Jesus as superior to
the Temple authorities. However, his focus is on who
is lost. At first glance it looks like Jesus is lost, but,
upon careful consideration, we begin to see that the
authorities are lost in amazement at Jesus' understanding and questions.

When something is lost we attempt to find it. So we
hunt for the lost car keys and find them in a purse, on
a table, or in a pocket. Coins are always falling between the sofa cushions, rolling under the refrigerator,
or disappearing into the floor vents; they are found by
those who clean the house. Usually, lost tools can be
found where they were last used. Because of our focus
on looking for lost things, we may never consider ourselves lost and in need of being found.

And that is the key to understanding the story of Jesus being lost in the Temple. See, he is not lost; the Spirit-child is in God's house on earth where he belongs. The Temple authorities are lost and his parents are lost. None of them understands what he is saying to them. Later in the Gospel, Luke will portray Jesus as grouping together and narrating three parables. One will be about a lost sheep, one about a lost coin, and one about a lost son. The sheep, coin, or son do not know it or he is lost. However, in all three stories each is found by someone, just like God searches and finds those who are lost.

The parables, like the story of Jesus lost in the Temple, make us aware that we, too, are lost. We cannot find God, no matter how hard we search; God finds us when we open ourselves to the possibility of being found by the Divine Presence. It might be in prayer, it might be in ranching, it might be in cleaning, it might be in family relationships that God finds us. We can get too distracted with thinking that we are the searchers, like the Temple authorities, instead of with waiting to be found by a God who loves to throw a party when what was lost has been found.

As you pray this mystery, reflect upon all the ways that God has found you through others. And be joyful that God seeks the lost.

The Mysteries of Light

The Baptism of Jesus in the Jordan

In those days Jesus came from Nazareth of Galilee and was baptized by John in the Jordan. (Mark 1:9)

The baptism of Jesus by John the Baptist in the Jordan River is the subject of many stained glass windows, paintings, mosaics, and baptismal font covers. In almost every depiction John pours water over the head of a standing or kneeling Jesus while a dove hovers above and rays of light pierce the clouds in the sky. However, not one of the four accounts of Jesus' baptism in the Jordan mentions most of that. While there is no doubt that John baptized Jesus in Mark's Gospel, he does it reluctantly in Matthew's Gospel (3:13-17); and he's already locked up in prison in Luke's Gospel (3:20), so we don't know who baptized Jesus (3:21-22). There is no portrayal of John baptizing Jesus in John's Gospel; all we have is the testimony of the Baptizer (1:29-34).

Because each evangelist after Mark, commonly accepted as the oldest Gospel, tries to tone down or erase Jesus' baptism by John, we must conclude that the event caused a problem near the end of the first century. Many were saying that John must be the greater since he did the baptizing. By gradually removing John from the scene, Matthew and Luke elevate Jesus. The author of John's Gospel deals with the issue by not even narrating the event. There is little doubt that John the Baptist baptized Jesus; if he hadn't, Matthew and Luke wouldn't have rewritten Mark's story.

In Mark's Gospel, after Jesus is baptized he sees the heavens torn apart and God descend to the earth like a dove. In the ancient three-storied universe, God lived on the top level (above the heavens). People lived on the middle floor (earth), and the dead lived on the first floor (under the earth). The torn-apart heavens, then, indicate that God has come to earth. Jesus alone hears the voice from heaven declare that he is its son in whom it is well pleased. Thus, it is no great revelation that Jesus begins his mission proclaiming, ". . . The kingdom of God has come near . . ." (Mark 1:15).

Today, the Mighty One's voice comes through human voices who, like Jesus, proclaim God's activity in our lives. As husbands and wives discern careers, children, buying a house, buying a car, they can hear the Holy One's voice. Parents are God's voice through the example of the lifestyle they model for their children. Friends who listen intently, give advice, or comfort serve as the voice of God. The Merciful One's revelation in our lives through others' voices often is like a beam of light. Suddenly, we recognize that God's reign has come near our lives.

As you pray this mystery of light, reflect on what God has been saying to you through all the enlightening voices in your life.

The Manifestation of Jesus
at the Wedding at Cana

Jesus did . . . the first of his signs, in Cana of Galilee,
and revealed his glory; and his disciples believed in him.
(John 2:11)

The unique narrative of the wedding at Cana is the first of Jesus' seven major signs in John's Gospel which spark belief in his disciples. The basic Johannine scenario for each of the signs involves an event, a miraculous deed done by Jesus, and the ensuing faith of those who are present. In the Gospels of Mark, Matthew, and Luke, people who come to Jesus already have faith; in John, they believe because they see Jesus' signs.

The wedding at Cana is no ordinary marriage. From the opening line of the story, indicating that it takes place "on the third day" (2:1), the astute reader knows this is a theophany, a manifestation of God through Jesus. No bride is mentioned, but the unnamed mother of Jesus is present; she is a sign of the church. And there are six stone water jars, an incomplete number.

In John's Gospel, this story begins Jesus' ministerial journey of revealing and wedding God to people that will reach a crescendo at the cross. There we find the unnamed mother of Jesus making her second and final appearance in the Gospel; there we find the missing seventh jar of wine; and there we find the church-bride, created from water and blood flowing out of the side of the new Adam, Christ. The cross weds heaven to earth; through the new Adam and his bride, God re-creates all. The wedding begun at Cana is completed on the cross. Thus, the wedding at Cana and the cross serve as covers for John's Gospel; what goes on in between is the gradual merger of God and people through Jesus.

The Johannine wedding metaphor can be employed by all who are on a pilgrimage to wholeness. It takes a lifetime to integrate or wed all our human aspects: mental, physical, sexual, psychological, emotional, and spiritual. But time and time again we get a glimpse of such wholeness in a mystic moment of wedded bliss. It may come after finishing a good book or a strenuous workout. It may appear after agonizing over and then solving a problem or understanding an emotional dilemma in a new way. Through each's sharing of self, a married man and woman enact wholeness in their lives. The individual feeling of wholeness is a sign that God is being revealed and more deeply wed to us in and through our lives

As you pray this mystery of light, reflect on the key moments of a wedding, when you have experienced wholeness, and, therefore, God, in your life.

The Proclamation
of the Kingdom of God

*[Jesus said,] "The kingdom of God is not coming with things
that can be observed; nor will they say, 'Look, here it is!' or
'There it is!' For, in fact, the kingdom of God is among you."*
(Luke 17:20-21)

It matters little how it is phrased; even though each
evangelist puts his own spin on Jesus' message that
"the kingdom of God has come near" (Mark 1:15), that
"the kingdom of heaven has come near" (Matt 4:16), or
that "the kingdom of God is among you" (Luke 17:21).
The basic concept that God is with people here and
now serves as Jesus' basic proclamation. No matter
which Gospel we read, we watch Jesus enact God's
reign primarily through parables, but also through
teachings, debates, exorcisms, healings, and other
deeds.

God is everywhere people are, declares Jesus. Such
is not a radical concept to us today. But for ancient
people who "located" God above the vault in the
heavens or in the Holy of Holies of the Temple, Jesus'
declaration that God is among them was very hard to
take. His preaching identified God's reign as present;
it is not some type of life to look forward to after
death. It is not some eternal reward or punishment.
God's reign is among us.

Of course, it is much easier to turn the presence of
God into a distant longing and tone down Jesus' basic
message. Despite the fact that people talk about seek-
ing God, they would often enough prefer that the
Always-present One stay out of their business. By

turning the proclamation of God's reign into a future event, churches are able to control their members by making them work toward and hope for a life beyond the grave.

However, God cannot be so controlled, even by technicians of the sacred. God's reign erupts like light from deep within us. When we see the injustice of a living wage and speak out against and work toward changing the system that keeps others locked in it, the reign of God is at hand. When we speak the truth in the midst of corporate stealing and lying and fraud, God's reign is near. Just treating every person with basic human dignity by refusing to engage in racism, sexism, or religionism reveals God's rule among us. In those special moments, we take over where Jesus left off and enact God's reign here and now. That is why Christianity is a way of life; it's the way one lives in the kingdom now instead of a plan of how to earn heaven. In other words, we live in God's now.

As he went about proclaiming God's reign, Jesus gathered followers who represented the kind of people in whom God was interested. The poor, prostitutes, tax collectors, lepers, the lost, inept fishermen, the diseased—they were ushered into God's reign. Throughout biblical history, these are the types of people God has favored for the Merciful One's kingdom. The interest continues today through those who continue to proclaim God's rule.

As you pray this mystery of light, reflect upon the times that God's kingdom has erupted from deep within you.

The Transfiguration

[Jesus] was transfigured before [Peter, James, and John], and his face shone like the sun, and his clothes became dazzling white. (Matt 17:2)

The account of Jesus' transfiguration occurs in Mark (9:2-13), Matthew (17:1-8), and Luke (9:28-36). In each Gospel the story of Jesus' metamorphosis has a different meaning, depending upon its location. For Mark, transfiguration is another way to attempt to describe resurrection; since the original ending of Mark gives no post-resurrection appearances of Jesus, Mark tells us that resurrection is like being changed into white light while speaking with the two long-dead heroes, Moses and Elijah and encountering the law and the prophet in a new and different way. Matthew alters the transfiguration narrative he found in Mark by envisioning it as a revelatory event of epic proportions predicting the post-resurrection appearances Jesus makes at the end of the Gospel. Luke, too, rewrites the story he found in Mark by seeing it as the epitome of Jesus' journey to Jerusalem, where he will make his exodus through death to perfect new life, and recording several post-resurrection appearances to prove that there is life on the other side of the grave.

Even though all three accounts of the transfiguration differ, they maintain one similarity. God did something through Jesus. Notice that the verb is always passive—Jesus was transfigured, not he transfigured himself. What each Synoptic Gospel writer describes as happening only once actually took place many times in Jesus' life. God's light shined through him, and Jesus cooperated with that light throughout his life. Mark portrays Jesus' understanding of his mission to change from one of preaching powerful words and doing mighty deeds to one of teaching the way of the powerless throughout his brief ministry. Matthew portrays Jesus as coming to see that his mission to the lost sheep of the house of Israel has to be expanded to the nations of the world. And in Luke, Jesus' journey to Jerusalem can't stop there. His mission must be delegated to the next generation of Gentiles after the evangelization efforts of the heroic apostles Peter and Paul.

God transfigures, sparks change, throughout your life. God's light breaks through in love shared and consecrated by husband and wife and all the interchange that occurs throughout their marriage. It shines through children and grandchildren, causing parents and grandparents to change their lives. The glow of a sunrise or sunset may evoke a transformation. Walking through a park, the woods, a meadow, or a flower garden can send a blare of beauty that leaves one altered. Even embers kindled in a fireplace can produce a brightness that fills one with insight and alters thought patterns.

As you pray this mystery of light, reflect on all the changes God has worked in your life and how God's brilliance has left you changed forever, never again to be the same. Be prepared, like Jesus, to be dazzled.

The Institution of the Eucharist

While [Jesus and his disciples] were eating, he took a loaf of bread, and after blessing it he broke it, gave it to them, and said, "Take; this is my body." Then he took a cup and after giving thanks he gave it to them, and all of them drank from it. He said to them, "This is my blood of the covenant, which is poured out for many." (Mark 14:22-24)

In the New Testament, there are four distinct versions of the Lord's Supper or the Institution of the Eucharist: Mark 14:22-25; Matthew 26:26-29; Luke 22:14-23; 1 Corinthians 11:23-26. Most Catholics are familiar with the narrative they hear in the eucharistic prayer during Mass. However, it is a synthesis of all four versions mentioned above.

Each portrayal reflects the biblical author's interpretation of the meaning of Jesus' death as viewed from the Jewish feast of Passover. Mark understands Jesus' death to be in continuity with the covenant God entered into with Moses through blood. Matthew declares that Jesus' death is for the forgiveness of sins. Both Luke and Paul say that Jesus' death creates a new covenant, like the one Jeremiah said would be written on people's hearts (Jer 31:31-33). John's Gospel substitutes the bread of life discourse in chapter 6 for a eucharistic institution account and portrays Jesus washing his disciples' feet as an example of service on the night before he died in chapter 13.

Even though the meaning of each version of the Lord's Supper is different, all four accounts feature the same common food staples of the ancient world: bread and wine. The bread would have been unleavened, coarse, round, flat loaves—not the vitamin-fortified, pre-sliced, packaged oblong blocks of today. The wine would have been little more than fermented grape juice cut with water—not a blood-red Merlot from France or a Shiraz from Australia. The result of people together eating bread and drinking wine—unity—is the reverse of the process of making those staples. Many individual grains of wheat are ground together to make flour. Many grapes are squeezed together to get juice to make wine. Just as the many grains become one loaf and the many grapes become one wine, so the many diners become one. In other words, when people eat and drink together, they enter into a unity that the Lord's Supper discloses as the real presence of God in Christ, both through the elements and through the diners.

We don't realize how often we enact this mystery, other than celebrating the Lord's Supper. When families and friends gather for Thanksgiving dinner, Christmas lunch, Easter brunch, and birthday and anniversary commemorations, they may eat turkey, ham, or roast, but the staples of bread and wine are present in some form. Through the action of eating and drinking together, the diners renew the ties that bind them together. When Jesus instituted the Eucharist, he established a tie that binds all people into his one family, the body of Christ.

As you pray this mystery of light, reflect on the unifying experiences you have had through the staples of bread and wine. And give thanks to God for them.

The Sorrowful Mysteries

The Agony in the Garden

[Jesus] began to be distressed and agitated. And he said to
[Peter, James, and John], "I am deeply grieved, even to death;
remain here, and keep awake." (Mark 14:33-34)

The account of Jesus' agony in the garden appears in
three Gospels: Mark 14:32-42; Matthew 26:36-46, and
Luke 22:39-46. Each evangelist writes about the scene
differently because each understands it to serve a different theological purpose. A distressed and agitated
Jesus prays three times in Gethsemane in Mark's
Gospel because the tragedy of his suffering and death
is quickly approaching. Likewise, a grieved and
agitated Jesus prays three times in Gethsemane in
Matthew's Gospel because he is about to be betrayed
by Judas. However, a sweating-blood Jesus prays but
once on the Mount of Olives in Luke's Gospel, which
mentions that an angel came to strengthen him as he
prepares for his innocent martyrdom. John's Gospel
doesn't mention an agony-in-the-garden scene because it would portray the divine Jesus as too human.
The accounts of the agony contain the common theme
that doing God's will involves suffering for Jesus—
and for us.

We spend a lot of time avoiding the suffering and
dying that are intricately attached to living. More
energy can be spent circumventing suffering and
dying than is needed to walk through them. So, we
procrastinate projects at home because doing them
means giving up some TV or movie time or some other
pleasurable activities. A relationship that's not mutu-
ally nourishing for both persons just continues rather

than one person facing the other and calling him or her to accountability. Employers complain that they get fewer hours of work from employees, who find more and more distractions, like cell phones, personal calls, days off, etc., because they don't face the work and finish it. Students in high school and college often put off homework and paper-writing until the last possible moment in an effort to avoid the agony of completing assignments.

The word "agony" means "anguish," "struggle," "intense pain." Being a human being, Jesus experiences anguish when faced with the prospect of his own suffering and death. He struggles to do God's will, and he experiences both the mental and the physical pain of dying on a cross. He serves as a model of how to face the agony and follow the path through it instead of finding ways to avoid it. He trusts that God's presence will sustain him through the agony and enrich his life because of it.

As you pray this sorrowful mystery, reflect on your own experiences both of putting off agony and going through it. In which ones did you experience the presence of God? How was your life enriched?

The Scourging at the Pillar

Pilate took Jesus and had him flogged. (John 19:1)

While each evangelist gives an account of Jesus being mocked in some manner, only John's Gospel says that he was flogged or scourged or whipped severely. This small detail in John becomes a very long scene in movies featuring Jesus' trial, like "Jesus of Nazareth," "Jesus," and "King of Kings." Moviemakers often exploit this element with lots of blood flowing out of gaping wounds on Jesus' back. The author of John's Gospel gives no details of the scourging; he doesn't even mention how it was accomplished. Based on what was common practice in the first century, a prisoner could have his clothes pulled off and his hands tied around a pillar or post. Then a man wielding a single whip or one with several leather strips with lead beads or shells attached to the ends proceeded to beat the prisoner either into submission or as punishment or to weaken him in preparation for death.

Forms of beating have existed throughout history. The "rule of thumb" in England originally referred to the size of the stick a husband could use to beat his wife; it could be no larger than his thumb. Today, we'd call it spouse abuse. In schools children were beaten often with rulers, yard sticks, paddles, or spanked. Often called "the board of education," the instrument was used to discipline unruly students. Today, we'd call it child abuse. Slaves who failed to live up to their master's expectations or who ran away were often tied to a post and whipped by their owner. And those who failed to complete an order or deserted any branch of the armed forces were often flogged by their commanding officer. Today, these would be lawsuits.

Such treatment repulses us, but it goes on nevertheless. It may not be a physical flogging that leaves whelps or wounds, but a verbal lashing by a spouse, teacher, or parent that can hurt psychologically: "I don't love you. I hate you. Get out of my life. You're good for nothing. You're stupid." Such verbal scourging takes longer to heal, if it ever does, and it leaves scars that often last a lifetime.

James has harsh words for those whose tongues need to be scourged: "If any think they are religious, and do not bridle their tongues but deceive their hearts, their religion is worthless" (1:26). Later he adds, "How great a forest is set ablaze by a small fire! And the tongue is a fire. The tongue is placed among our members as a world of iniquity; it stains the whole body, sets on fire the cycle of nature, and is itself set on fire by hell" (3:5b-6).

As you pray this mystery, reflect on the verbal scourgings you have given to others, make a promise to discipline your tongue, and, sorrowfully, ask God for help to avoid future tongue lashings.

The Crowning with Thorns

[The soldiers] clothed [Jesus] in a purple cloak; and after twisting some thorns into a crown, they put it on him.
(Mark 15:17)

We have a tendency to focus on the thorns in this mystery. Many Good Friday crosses display wreaths of thorny rose-bush branches or large needles from a wild thorn tree. We would do better to look at the crown and the cloak accompanying it in the Gospels. Mark's Gospel says that the Roman soldiers dress Jesus in a crown of thorns and a purple cloak. Matthew's Gospel declares that the Roman soldiers put a scarlet robe on Jesus along with the crown (27:28-29). Luke mentions neither. And John's Gospel first mentions the crown of thorns and then the purple robe (19:2). The evangelists portray truth emerging from irony. Jesus is crowned king and hailed as such by the Roman occupation forces of Palestine. He is dressed in either royal purple or a scarlet Roman military cloak. His crown depicts him as an emperor, since Roman emperors are often depicted on coins and reliefs wearing a laurel wreath crown of victory. With a reed for a scepter and the soldiers declaration, "Hail, King of the Jews!"—echoing the "Hail, Caesar!" of the ancient Romans—the truth in the irony of Jesus' kingship is complete.

Jesus rules from a position of powerlessness, and that is what gives him his kingship. Emperors and kings rule by power and lineage, but Jesus reigns as servant. He is not interested in the control or manipulation of others. His ministry is one of care for others. So, he is ironically crowned by the very forces responsible for his death, and Jesus wields his powerless kingship to set free all who are oppressed, even the oppressors.

Some people create their crowns out of the success of trampling over others to get ahead. Others fashion crowns through the control they exert with language that provokes feelings of guilt and remorse. Through their manipulation of others, some weave a crown of poor choices with horrible consequences. Others form crowns by visiting the sick, holding the hands of the dying, tutoring students, raising other peoples' kids, being a good neighbor, and ministering in one's church. Looking carefully, we see that they can be either invisible crowns of thorns or crowns of service. Matthew's Gospel portrays Jesus identifying himself with those who are hungry, thirsty, strangers, naked, sick, and imprisoned, saying to those who did the right thing because it was the right thing to do: "Just as you did it to one of the least of these who are members of my family, you did it to me" (25:40).

As you pray this sorrowful mystery of Jesus being crowned with thorns, reflect on your crown. Is it a crown of thorns or one of powerless service to others?

The Carrying of the Cross

As [the Roman soldiers] led [Jesus] away, they seized a man,
Simon of Cyrene, who was coming from the country, and they
laid the cross on him, and made him carry it behind Jesus.
(Luke 23:26)

As in the scourging scene in movies about Jesus, he
usually struggles to carry his cross to the hill of crucifixion. Most of the time Jesus is seen carrying a cross
formed from two heavy beams of timber that resemble
railroad ties. However, only John's Gospel (19:17) portrays Jesus as carrying his cross alone; the One who
claims to be God, saying "I AM," needs no help to
complete his work. Both Mark (15:21) and Matthew
(27:32) say that Simon of Cyrene carried Jesus' cross;
thus, Jesus didn't carry it. Luke adjusts the text to
disclose his understanding that discipleship means
following behind Jesus; thus, Simon of Cyrene carries
Jesus' cross behind him.

Whoever carried Jesus' cross probably hauled only
the crossbeam to the place of crucifixion. The upright
post stayed in place and the crossbeam fitted over it.
While it was customary for a condemned man to carry
his own crossbeam in order to further humiliate him
and turn the capital punishment event into a public
spectacle in order to intimidate others, those weak-
ened by scourging, hunger, or dehydration needed
assistance.

The gospel writers cannot agree on how Jesus and
his cross got to Golgotha, The Place of the Skull, because they are interested in teaching discipleship.
They want to give the reader an understanding of

what it means to follow Jesus. No evangelist paints a pretty picture of discipleship, especially insofar as it entails denying self, taking the cross, following Jesus, and enduring persecution. But that was the reality of the last third of the first century common era for those first disciples of Jesus of Nazareth. While we might prefer crosses with wheels on them today, in the past many discovered death because they were followers of Jesus.

In some countries, Christians are still persecuted. But in most of the world crosses are few and far between. Diseases, like cancer and AIDS, for which no cure has yet been found, are crosses. Those in automobile, plane, train, climbing, and swimming accidents may carry the cross of healing and/or irreparable damage of some kind. Trauma, abuse, and the unwillingness to forgive can be counted among the psychological crosses some people tote. The emotional strains of marriage and child-rearing are crosses parents carry. No matter what the burden, the focus must be on discipleship. The question is always this: How well do we carry our crosses throughout the living of our lives?

As you pray this sorrowful mystery, reflect on both the crosses you have carried and those you now carry and how those illustrate your understanding of discipleship.

The Crucifixion

When [the Roman soldiers] had crucified [Jesus], they divided
his clothes among thesmelves by casting lots. . . .
(Matt 27:35)

The Romans often followed a master plan when de-
signing a new city. One main street would run north
and south and the other one would bisect it east and
west. Thus, the city would be divided into four quad-
rants, forming what the Romans thought of as order.
The two main streets bisecting each other formed a
cross. Anyone who caused disorder, such as murderers
and traitors, were put to death on the instrument rep-
resenting order: a cross. Those who caused chaos in
the orderly city were crucified, and their crucifixion
served as a deterrent for anyone thinking of disturbing
the *pax Romana* or peace of Rome.

The Gospels do not describe crucifixion because the
original audience knew about the variety of ways it was
done. Seldom did the Romans put to death a single
criminal; they preferred a large group of men so as to
make a bigger public spectacle. After stripping the
prisoner naked in order to humiliate him as much as
possible, nails were usually driven through his wrists
—not hands—and feet. He may or may not also be tied
at the arms to the crossbeam for support, and a small
wooden footrest might be nailed below his feet to give
him leverage. The goal of crucifixion was not to kill the
criminal quickly, but to prolong his suffering as long as
possible. Some of the crucified hung alive on their
crosses for days, exposed to the elements and wild
animals, before finally succumbing to asphyxiation.

While we don't employ the Roman form of capital punishment today, we have found other ways to crucify people. The electric chair may still be used in some places, but a lethal injection is more sterile and causes less of a spectacle with viewers seated behind a window in a theater-like room. Besides such deadly crucifixions there are the non-deadly ones each of us manages to impose on others. For example, we refuse to relinquish the old image of a person as an alcoholic, drug abuser, or street person no matter how much he or she has changed. In national, state, local, office, and home politics, leaders crucify each other on economic, war, domestic, and foreign policy issues. Sexism and racism can be the cross that forces one out of a job so the boss does not have to fire him or her. Our ways of crucifying may be more humane, but the result is the same: the denigration of a human being at his or her expense.

As you pray this mystery, reflect on the crucifixions in which you have taken part and sorrowfully ask God for forgiveness.

The Glorious Mysteries

The Resurrection

Very early on the first day of the week, when the sun had risen, [Mary Magdalene and Mary the Mother of James and Salome] went to the tomb. . . . When they looked up, they saw that the stone, which was very large, had . . . been rolled back. (Mark 16:2, 4)

Strictly speaking, there are no eye-witness accounts of Christ's resurrection in the New Testament because resurrection is a statement of faith that cannot be proved. Mark's Gospel says that three women found the tomb's stone rolled away and a young man seated on the right side (16:1-8). Adding the apocalyptic drama of an earthquake, Matthew's Gospel declares that two women watched an angel roll back the stone and sit upon it (28:1-10). Luke's Gospel portrays spice-bearing women finding the open tomb without a body but with the appearance of two men in dazzling clothes (24:1-13). Mary Magdalene discovers the open tomb in John's Gospel and runs to tell Simon Peter and the beloved disciple, both of whom race to the tomb (20:1-10).

The empty tomb, no matter how it is described, is a metaphor for resurrection, but the empty tomb does not prove resurrection. If you were walking through a cemetery and saw an opening, you would reach one of the following conclusions: (1) someone was going to be buried there, (2) someone had robbed a grave, or (3) someone had been exhumed. You would not conclude that someone had been raised from the dead. We don't know what resurrection from the dead means because it is on the other side of death, and we have no knowledge of what reality is like over there. That is why it is easier to explain resurrection by saying that it is not resuscitation, but it is like an empty tomb or a bodiless body that can appear and disappear (see Luke's [24:13-53] and John's [20:11–21:25] post-resurrection stories).

Each evangelist believes that God raised Jesus from the dead and assigns a meaning to that statement of faith. For Mark, resurrection means that God does not abandon faithful people in death even when they think such is the case. For Matthew, resurrection means that God guarantees life for the righteous through death. Discipleship involves witnessing suffering and death before resurrection in Luke. And in John, resurrection means that seeing is not always believing—but sometimes it is. In general, each Gospel writer attempts to make clear that resurrection is the "something more" of reality that we experience throughout our lives.

While loving and raising children, parents often say that there must be something more; they discover it in their adult children and grandchildren. Teachers in schools discover it in their former students who thank them for something the instructor has long forgotten. After a long day, white, blue, and no collar workers discover the something more when they are told that they did a good job. That "something more" to life is a glimpse of the reality of resurrection.

As you pray this mystery, recall some of your glorious resurrection experiences of something more.

The Ascension

While [Jesus] was blessing [his disciples], he withdrew from them and was carried up into heaven. (Luke 24:51)

In Luke's Gospel the risen Jesus makes several post-resurrection appearances on Easter Sunday before he ascends from Bethany that same evening. However, in Luke's second volume, the Acts of the Apostles, the risen Jesus appears to his apostles during forty days (1:3) before he is lifted up from Mount Olivet (1:1-11). The author knows that a story does not have to be factual in order to communicate truth. Thus, in either scenario, the author has two purposes: (1) to remove the risen Jesus from the story and (2) to narrate the mission to Jews and Gentiles. In other words, the risen Jesus has to disappear for the mission to be enacted according to the Lukan theological schema. If he remains, then he, instead of the apostles, would be entrusted with the mission of spreading the Good News to the ends of the world.

For Luke, ascension is nothing other than resurrection in disguise. The same two men in dazzling clothes appear to the women at the tomb (Luke 24:4) and to the apostles after the ascension (Acts 1:10). In either scenario, the two men announce a vision. They challenge their hearers to open wide their eyes, to see the big picture, to get out of their little box of reality, and to look at the world and its universes from God's perspective. In effect, that is the challenge of the mission—witnessing to God's work throughout the world.

Sometimes the insights of children prove them to be wiser than adults; their view of reality is broader.

Those who have suffered through such diseases as cancer or undergone transplant surgery often communicate a deeper appreciation for life and death; their vision has been enlarged. When we are open consciously to the multitude of possibilities of living, we may experience ourselves being lifted above the dailyness of existence to see today as just one tiny, disappearing speck on the edge of the horizon. Travel to foreign countries often leaves the pilgrim with alternate ways of believing. A book may reveal an insight that moves the reader into depths of truth never before contemplated. Those and other countless times of change in our lives enable us to ascend, to get ourselves out of our little picture, and to embrace the big mission of being sent into the world to make it aware of the presence of God.

As you pray this mystery, reflect on your own glorious ascension experiences and thank God for sending you on the mission of sharing Good News.

The Descent of the Holy Spirit

While Peter was . . . speaking, the Holy Spirit fell upon all who heard the word. The circumcised believers . . . were astounded that the gift of the Holy Spirit had been poured out even on the Gentiles. . . . (Acts 10:44-45)

Almost everyone is familiar with the traditional story of Pentecost in the Acts of the Apostles. It features a violent wind, tongues of fire, and speaking in foreign languages (Acts 2:1-4). However, most people are not aware that there is another story of Pentecost in the Acts. The one in chapter 2 is the Jewish Pentecost; however, the one in chapter 10 is the Gentile Pentecost. The author of both accounts, Luke, is the first evangelist to develop an understanding of the Holy Spirit, theologically referred to as pneumatology. Luke declares that the Holy Spirit both launches and guides the mission of Jesus' apostles to the Jews and the Gentiles. He depicts Pentecost as a theophany, a manifestation of God in wind, like creation; in fire, like Sinai; and in languages, like Babel, that occurs fifty days after Jesus' resurrection. While there is less fanfare in chapter 10, once the Spirit descends upon the centurion Cornelius and his household, all are baptized in the name of Jesus Christ (Acts 10:48).

The author of John's Gospel portrays the post-resurrected Jesus appearing to, breathing on, and giving the Holy Spirit to his disciples on Easter Sunday evening (John 20:22). John understands the Holy Spirit to be Jesus returned (theologically called realized eschatology); that's why the author often refers to the Spirit as the Advocate, Paraclete, or Comforter. Like

God breathed life into Adam, Jesus breathes life into his huddled-together band of followers, who are sent to preach that Jesus is the Messiah, the Son of God, through whom people may have life.

The metaphors for the Holy Spirit—wind, fire, tongues, and breath—that worked for Luke and John continue for us today. The gathering of family and friends for birthdays, anniversaries, Thanksgiving, and Christmas reminds all of the ties that bind them into one; there is a definite Spirit present as language discloses stories of suffering, tales of exploration, and narratives of experiences by young and old alike. A quiet walk in the park or woods might reveal a tree on fire with fall colors or the sunrise or sunset igniting the sky. A puff of air rattles the wind chimes and reveals the invisible presence of God's Spirit. Just taking a deep breath can remind us of the newness we experience every time we inhale and exhale.

As you pray this mystery, reflect on some of your life's Pentecosts, those glorious Spirit-experiences of wind, fire, language, and breath.

The Assumption

Christ has been raised from the dead, the first fruits of those who have died. For since death came through a human being, the resurrection of the dead has also come through a human being. (1 Cor 15:20-21)

The doctrine of the Virgin Mary's assumption into heaven, also referred to as the Dormition, is not a biblical event. It can be understood only from the perspective of the doctrine of the Immaculate Conception, the belief that Mary was preserved free from all stain of original sin, and from the belief that Jesus Christ, true God and true man, free of all sin, was raised from the dead by God. What is believed about Mary is based on what is believed about Christ. Thus, if Jesus is sinless and the Mighty One raised him from the dead, the logical conclusion is that Mary, his mother (the Mother of God), who was sinless, would also have to be raised from the dead by the Holy One. The assumption of Mary is her participation in Christ's resurrection and serves as a foreshadowing of what awaits those who follow her Son. In other words, Mary's assumption represents the hope for new life on the other side of the grave for all who wait.

In his First Letter to the Corinthians, Paul establishes the basis for this belief. He argues that there have been two Adams—the original one God created who sinned and brought death into the world and the second one, Christ, through whom God recreated and brought life into the world via the resurrection. Later, in his letter, Paul quotes the saying, "Death has been swallowed up in victory" (15:54). In other words, the death brought by the first Adam has been eaten alive by the resurrection of the second Adam. Mary, the mother of the second Adam, is the second human being to experience resurrection because she, like her Son, was not subject to the death that was the result of the first Adam's disobedience. Because of her waiting in obedience to God, she has been assumed into heaven.

Mary's assumption represents what awaits those who hope for the day when "God may be all in all" (1 Cor 15:28). She models what God can do in those who wait in faith, hope, and love for the Merciful One to act. You may be waiting for a new job or for a ride somewhere. You may be waiting for the birth of a child or for the paperwork for an adoption to be completed. You may be waiting for a letter in the mail or a friend or family member to arrive for a visit. Any time that you wait in faith, hope, and love, you imitate Mary's waiting for God to act in her life. Her assumption is our guarantee that God raises to new life those who wait for the Holy One to act.

As you pray this mystery, reflect on the glorious deeds God has done in your life while you wait.

The Coronation of the
Blessed Virgin Mary

*A great portent appeared in heaven: a woman clothed with
the sun, with the moon under her feet, and on her head a
crown of twelve stars.* (Rev 12:1)

Mary's exaltation and crowning by Christ as queen
of heaven, like her assumption, is not a biblical event.
It can be understood only from the perspective of the
doctrine of the Immaculate Conception, the belief that
Mary was preserved free from all stain of original sin,
and from the doctrine of the Assumption, that she was
assumed body and soul into heaven. What is believed
about Mary is based on what is believed about Christ.
Thus, if Jesus is the king of kings through his resurrection from the dead by God, Mary, his mother, would
have to be the queen through her assumption into
heaven by the Mighty One. Thus, her coronation con-
forms the Mother of God even more closely to the
image of Christ.

Apocalyptic literature, like that found in the book of
Revelation, attempts to depict this truth using a portent, a foreshadowing or omen written in signs or
codes. The woman, the personification of Israel, from
whom God brings forth the Messiah, is the incarnation
of the dream of Jacob's son, Joseph, who sees the sun
and moon and eleven stars bow to him. Israel is preg-
nant with and gives birth to the Messiah in the person
of Mary of Nazareth, chosen by God from all eternity
to be the mother of the Holy One's Son, Jesus Christ,
"a male child, who is to rule all the nations with a rod
of iron" (Rev 12:5). Mary's coronation represents the

crowning of her absolute cooperation with God in the plan of salvation.

Even though today there are few royals, kings and queens, nevertheless, people look at them as a little above the commoners. We expect them to be above any ethical reproach. As contestants in beauty pageants, we want the winning queen to be flawless in poise, conversation, and song. In the old "Queen for a Day" TV show, a woman won prizes and a crown for her ability to answer questions correctly. What we look for in queens of any kind is what the Mighty One found in Mary, whom the Holy One selected to be the mother of God's own Son.

Through baptism, we, too, have been chosen. After dying and rising with Christ, we were anointed, "Christed," with chrism oil and declared to be royal, chosen by God to cooperate with the Divine in the plan of salvation. We exercise our royal status, like Mary, when we discern and affirm God's work in our lives. It may not entail giving birth to the Messiah, but feeding the hungry, giving drink to the thirsty, clothing the naked, and visiting those in prison are royal activities nevertheless.

As you pray this glorious mystery, reflect on your exercise of your royal status and look for traces of God's plan in your life.